Funniest Verses of Ogden Nash

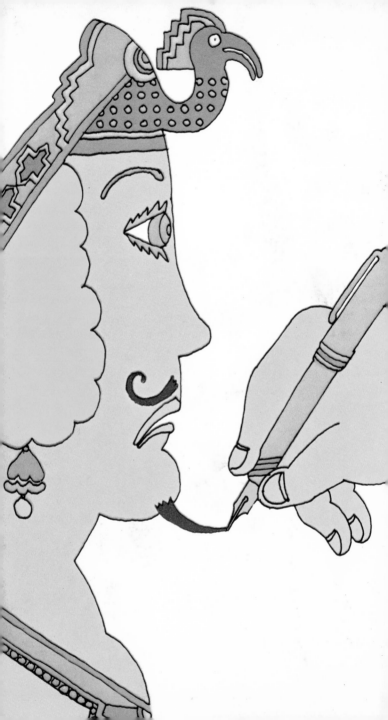

FUNNIEST VERSES
OF OGDEN NASH

Light Lyrics by One
of America's Favorite Humorists
Illustrated by Seymour Chwast
Selected by Dorothy Price

♛ Hallmark Editions

Funniest Verses of Ogden Nash

Kindly allow me to be your tutor.
I wish to explain about the commuter.
He rises so early and abrupt
That the robins complain he wake them upped.
Commuters think nothing could be more beautiful
Than the happy hours of the life commutiful,
But as one who tried it and now repentest,
I'd rather go twice a day to the dentist.
You struggle into the city's strife
With a shopping list from your thoughtful wife.
You repeat to yourself, as the day begins:
One charlotte russe; dozen bobby pins—
And then on the homeward trip you find
That this trifling chore has slipped your mind,
And the brilliantest explanation is useless
When you're bobby-pinless and charlotte russeless.
Let me add, to conclude this pitiful ditty,
A commuter is one who never knows how a show
    comes out because he has to leave early to catch
    a train to get him back to the country in time to
    catch a train to bring him back to the city.

In this foolish world there is nothing more numerous
Than different people's senses of humorous,
And the difference between different sense of humors
Is as wide as the gap between shorts and bloomers.
This is what humor boils down unto—
Are you him who doeth, or him who it's done to?
If a friend is dogged by some awful hoodoo,
Why, naturally, he doesn't laugh, but you do;
If the puppy is sick on your new Tuxedo,
Why, naturally, you don't laugh, but he do.
Humor depends on the point of view,
It's a question of what is happening to who;
It's a question facing which I surrender,
It's also a question of What's your gender?
Strong men have squandered the best of their life
In trying to coax a smile from their wife.
I know a wag named Septimus Best;
His wife won't laugh at his merriest jest.
Under her bed he hides a skeleton;
He fills her bathtub with glue and gelatin;
He draws whiskers on pictures of Cleopatra,
And he's disrespectful to Frank Sinatra;
And she just sits in her gown of taffeta
And refuses to smile, either during or afeter.
I guess a sense of humor is what
Husbands tell each other their wives haven't got.

I love coffee, I love tea,
I love the girls, but they're mean to me.
I love Saturday, I love Sunday,
But how could anyone ever love Monday?
Let's make a scientific analysis,
Let's diagnose this Monday paralysis.
Well, you've suffered an overdose of sunburn;
You must blister and peel before you un-burn.
For junk your muscles could all be sold for,
From engaging in games you are now too old for.
You're bloated from a diet of buns and hamburgers,
Chickenburgers, cheeseburgers, nutburgers,
    clamburgers.
Your hair may be brushed, but your mind's untidy,
You've had about seven hours' sleep since Friday,
No wonder you feel that lost sensation;
You're sunk from a riot of relaxation.
What you do on week ends, you claim to adore it.
But Monday's the day that you suffer for it.
That's why Labor Day is a red-letter news day—
Blue Monday doesn't come until Tuesday.

THE ABOMINABLE SNOWMAN

I've never seen an abominable snowman,
I'm hoping not to see one,
I'm also hoping, if I do,
That it will be a wee one.

CELERY

Celery, raw,
Develops the jaw,
But celery, stewed,
Is more quietly chewed.

NATURE ABHORS A VACANCY

An ordeal of which I easily tire
Is that of having a lease expire.
Where to unearth another residence?
You can't have the White House,
   that's the President's.
You scour the Bowery, ransack the Bronx,
Through funeral parlors and honky-tonks.
From river to river you comb the town
For a place to lay your family down.
You find one, you start to hoist your pennant,
And you stub your toe on the previous tenant.
He's in bed with croup, his children have gout,
And you can't push in until they pull out,
And when they pull out, the painters take on
And your date with the movers has come and gone,
So your furniture in storage sits
While you camp out royally at the Ritz.
When leases expire, one wish I've got,
To be a landlord, and live on a yacht.

THE PEOPLE UPSTAIRS

The people upstairs all practice ballet.
Their living room is a bowling alley.
Their bedroom is full of conducted tours.
Their radio is louder than yours.
They celebrate week ends all the week.
When they take a shower, your ceilings leak.
They try to get their parties to mix
By supplying their guests with Pogo sticks,
And when their orgy at last abates,
They go to the bathroom on roller skates.
I might love the people upstairs wondrous
If instead of above us, they just lived under us.

GLOSSINA MORSITANS, OR, THE TSETSE

A Glossina morsitans bit rich Aunt Betsy.
Tsk tsk, tsetse.

THE ABSENTEES

I'd ride a cock horse to Banbury Cross
For giblet gravy and cranberry sauce,
Two treats which are held in reserve by the waiter
Till you've finished your turkey and mashed potater.

NEXT!

I thought that I would like to see
The early world that used to be,
That mastodonic mausoleum,
The Natural History Museum.
Newspaper full of physicists,
I dropped my head upon my fists.
On iron seat in marble bower,
I slumbered through the closing hour.
At midnight in the vasty hall
The fossils gathered for a ball.
High above notices and bulletins
Loomed up the Mesozoic skeletons.
Aroused by who knows what elixirs,
They ground along like concrete mixers.
They bowed and scraped in reptile pleasure,
And then began to tread the measure.
There were no drums or saxophones,
But just the clatter of their bones,
A rolling, rattling carefree circus
Of mammoth polkas and mazurkas.
Pterodactyls and brontosauruses
Sang ghostly prehistoric choruses.
Amid the megalosauric wassail
I caught the eye of one small fossil.
Cheer up, old man, he said, and winked—
It's kind of fun to be extinct.

TABLEAU AT TWILIGHT

I sit in the dusk. I am all alone.
Enter a child and an ice-cream cone.

A parent is easily beguiled
By sight of this coniferous child.

The friendly embers warmer gleam,
The cone begins to drip ice cream.

Cones are composed of many a vitamin.
My lap is not the place to bitamin.

Although my raiment is not chinchilla,
I flinch to see it become vanilla.

Coniferous child, when vanilla melts
I'd rather it melted somewhere else.

Exit child with remains of cone.
I sit in the dusk.   I am all alone,

Muttering spells like an angry Druid,
Alone, in the dusk, with the cleaning fluid.

WHEN YOU SAY THAT, SMILE!
OR, ALL RIGHT THEN, DON'T SMILE

When the odds are long,
And the game goes wrong,
Does your joie de vivre diminish?
Have you little delight
In an uphill fight?
Do you wince at a Garrison finish?
Then here's my hand, my trusty partner!
I've always wanted a good disheartener.
Oh, things are frequently what they seem
and this is wisdom's crown:
only the game fish swims upstream,
but the sensible fish swims down.

Well, how is your pulse
When a cad insults
The lady you're cavaliering?
Are you willing to wait
To retaliate
Till the cad is out of hearing?
Then here's my hand, my trusty companion,
And may neither one of us fall in a canyon.
For things are frequently what they seem,
and this is wisdom's crown:
only the game fish swims upstream,
but the sensible fish swims down.

PRAYER AT THE END OF A ROPE

Dear Lord, observe this bended knee,
This visage meek and humble,
And heed this confidential plea,
Voiced in a reverent mumble.

I ask no miracles nor stunts,
No heavenly radiogram;
I only beg for once, just once,
To not be in a jam.

One little moment thy servant craves
Of being his own master;
One placid vale between the waves
Of duty and disaster.

Oh, when the postman's whistle shrills,
Just once, Lord, let me grin:
Let me have settled last month's bills
Before this month's come in.

Let me not bite more off the cob
Than I have teeth to chew;
Please let me finish just one job
Before the next is due.

Consider, too, my social life,
Sporadic though it be;
Why is it only mental strife
That pleasure brings to me?

For months, when people entertain,
Me they do not invite;
Then suddenly invitations rain,
All for the self-same night.

R.S.V.P.'s I pray thee send
Alone and not in bunches,
Or teach me I cannot attend
Two dinners or two lunches.

Let me my hostess not insult,
Not call her diamonds topaz;
Else harden me to the result
Of my fantastic faux pas.

One little lull, Lord, that's my plea,
Then loose the storm again;
Just once, this once, I beg to be
Not in a jam. Amen.

LINES ON FACING FORTY

I have a bone to pick with Fate.
Come here and tell me, girlie,
Do you think my mind is maturing late,
Or simply rotted early?

CHACUN À SON BERLITZ

French is easy.
At speaking French I am the champ of the
    Champs Elysees,
And since I can speak Parisian without a flaw,
I will tell you why the crows, or les corbeaux,
    always win their battle against the scarecrows:
    it's on account of their esprit de caw.

I'LL TAKE THE
HIGH ROAD COMMISSION

In between the route marks
And the shaving rhymes,
Black and yellow markers
Comment on the times.

All along the highway
Hear the signs discourse:
Men
SLOW
Working
;

Saddle
CROSSING
Horse

Cryptic crossroad preachers
Proffer good advice,

Helping wary drivers
Keep out of Paradise.

Transcontinental sermons,
Transcendental talk:

Soft
CAUTION
Shoulders
;

Cross
CHILDREN
Walk

Wisest of their proverbs,
Truest of their talk,
Have I found that dictum:
Cross
CHILDREN
Walk

When Adam took the highway
He left his sons a guide:
Cross
CHILDREN
Walk
;

Cheerful
CHILDREN
Ride

FAHRENHEIT GESUNDHEIT

Nothing is glummer
Than a cold in the summer.
A summer cold
Is to have and to hold.
A cough in the fall
Is nothing at all,
A winter snuffle
Is lost in the shuffle,
And April sneezes
Put leaves on the treeses,
But a summer cold
Is to have and to hold
Though golf course and beach
Slip beyond your reach,
By a fate grotesque
You can get to your desk,
And there is no rescue
From this germ grotesque,
You can feel it coming
In your nasal plumbing,
But there is no plumber
For a cold in the summer,
Nostrilly, tonsilly,
It prowls irresponsilly;
In your personal firmament
Its abode is permanent.

Oh, would it were curable
Rather than durable;
Were it Goering's or Himmler's,
Or somebody simlar's!
O Laval, were it thine!
But it isn't, it's mine.
A summer cold
Is to have and to hold.

MAYBE YOU CAN'T TAKE IT WITH YOU
BUT LOOK WHAT HAPPENS WHEN
YOU LEAVE IT BEHIND

As American towns and cities I wander through,
One landmark is constant everywhere I roam;
The house that the Banker built in nineteen-two,
Dim neon tells me is now a funeral home.

TO THE CHILD
WHO'S FARTHER FROM THE MANNERS
OR HOW TO BE YOUNG GRACEFULLY

Having reached the sixth of those Seven Ages,
I consider myself one of Nature's sages,
And, mumbling around my remaining tooth,
Recommend a few rules of thumb to youth.
Let's begin, as I believe we can,
With the motto, Manners makyth man.
The corollary we can't escape,
That lack of manners makyth ape.
Child, you may not be an Endymion
But neither need you be a Simian,
Learn to accept the facts of life,
Even from your father and his wife,
Who you'll one day find were in the groove,
And, as of now, have more sense than you've.
One fact as actual as hunger
Is that older people know more than younger;
Whatever you face, they've been all through it;
Give heed when they tell you how not to do it.
They also control, for better or worse,
Strings if not of the apron, still the purse,
And if your ear I may whisper a word to,
Your elders appreciate being deferred to.
They don't appreciate yahoo whoops,
Or sidewalk monopolizing groups,

They don't appreciate costumes sloppy,
No matter which brand of Brando you copy,
Or finding themselves, at the prandial board,
Either interrupted or ignored.
They know if you go too soon too steady
You'll join them as parents before you're ready.
Though you've grown too old for your elders
   to spank you,
They like the sound of Please and Thank You.
It's not a sign of approaching senility
When they try to teach you common civility;
The civil youngster's chance is a stronger one
For not only a better life, but a longer one,
Since the driver who with Death is the flirtiest
Is the rudest, raucousest, and discourtiest,
One even Pravda could hardly applaud,
A nuisance at home and a boor abroad.
Don't sneer, or reject my words grimacefully,
I append the secret of being young gracefully;
The recipe calls for two ingredients:
Thoughtfulness and, alas, obedience.
Follow this, and you'll hear your parents purr,
For you'll be the marvel they think they were.

ASK DADDY, HE WON'T KNOW

Now that they've abolished chrome work
I'd like to call their attention to home work.
Here it is only three decades since my scholarship
   was famous,
And I'm an ignoramus.
I cannot think which goes sideways and
   which goes up and down, a parallel or a meridian,
Nor do I know the name of him who first translated
   the Bible into Indian, I see him only as
   an enterprising colonial Gideon.
I have difficulty with dates,
To say nothing of the annual rainfall
   of the Southern Central States.
Naturally the correct answers are just back
   of the tip of my tongue,
But try to explain that to your young.
I am overwhelmed by their erudite banter,
I am in no condition to differentiate
   between Tamerlane and Tam O'Shanter.
I reel, I sway, I am utterly exhausted;
Should you ask me when Chicago was founded
   I could only reply I didn't even know
   it was losted.

AND HOW KEEN WAS THE VISION OF SIR LAUNFAL?

Man's earliest pastime, I suppose,
Was to play with his fingers and his toes.
Then later, wearying of himself,
He devised the monster and the elf,
Enlivening his existence drab
With Blunderbore and Puck and Mab.
A modern man, in modern Maryland,
I boast my private gate to fairyland,
My kaleidoscope, my cornucopia,
My own philosopher's stone, myopia.
Except when rationalized by lenses,
My world is not what other men's is;
Unless I have my glasses on,
The postman is a leprechaun,
I can wish on either of two new moons,
Billboards are graven with mystic runes,
Shirts hung to dry are ragtag gypsies,
Mud puddles loom like Mississipsies,
And billiard balls resemble plums,
And street lamps are chrysanthemums.
If my vision were twenty-twenty,
I should miss miracles aplenty.

OH, PLEASE DON'T GET UP!

There is one form of life to which I unconditionally
    surrender,
Which is the feminine gender.
I think there must be some great difference
    in the way men and women are built,
Because women walk around all day wearing shoes
      that a man would break his neck the first step
      he took in them because where a man's shoe has
      a heel a woman's shoe has a stilt.
Certainly a man shod like a woman would just have
    to sit down all day, and yet my land!
Women not only don't have to sit, but prefer to stand,
Because their pleasure in standing up is exquisite,
As everybody knows who has ever watched a woman
    pay a call or a visit,
Because the proportions of feminine social chitchat
    are constant, always;
One part of sitting down in the sitting room
    to four parts standing up saying good-by
    in foyers and hallways,
Which is why I think that when it comes
    to physical prowess,
Why woman is a wow, or should I say a wowess.

ASSORTED CHOCOLATES

If some confectioner were willing
To let the shape announce the filling,
We'd encounter fewer assorted chocs,
Bitten into and returned to the box.

TIN WEDDING WHISTLE

Though you know it anyhow
Listen to me, darling, now,

Proving what I need not prove
How I know I love you, love.

Near and far, near and far,
I am happy where you are;

Likewise I have never learnt
How to be it where you aren't.

Far and wide, far and wide,
I can walk with you beside;

Furthermore, I tell you what,
I sit and sulk where you are not.

Visitors remark my frown
When you're upstairs and I am down,

Yes, and I'm afraid I pout
When I'm indoors and you are out;

But how contentedly I view
Any room containing you.

In fact I care not where you be,
Just as long as it's with me.

In all your absences I glimpse
Fire and flood and trolls and imps.

Is your train a minute slothful?
I goad the stationmaster wrothful.

When with friends to bridge you drive
I never know if you're alive,

And when you linger late in shops
I long to telephone the cops.

Yet how worth the waiting for,
To see you coming through the door.

Somehow, I can be complacent
Never but with you adjacent.

Near and far, near and far,
I am happy where you are;

Likewise, I have never learnt
How to be it where you aren't.

Then grudge me not my fond endeavor,
To hold you in my sight forever;

Let none, not even you, disparage
Such valid reason for a marriage.

A WATCHED EXAMPLE NEVER BOILS

The weather is so very mild
That some would call it warm.
Good gracious, aren't we lucky, child?
Here comes a thunderstorm.

The sky is now indelible ink,
The branches reft asunder;
But you and I, we do not shrink;
We love the lovely thunder.

The garden is a raging sea,
The hurricane is snarling;
Oh happy you and happy me!
Isn't the lightning darling?

Fear not the thunder, little one.
It's weather, simply weather;
It's friendly giants full of fun
Clapping their hands together.

I hope of lightning our supply
Will never be exhausted;
You know it's lanterns in the sky
For angels who are losted.

We love the kindly wind and hail,
The jolly thunderbolt,
We watch in glee the fairy trail
Of ampere, watt, and volt.

Oh, than to enjoy a storm like this
There's nothing I would rather.
Don't dive beneath the blankets, Miss!
Or else leave room for Father.

THE VOLUBLE WHEEL CHAIR

When you roll along admiring the view,
And everyone drives too fast but you;
When people not only ignore your advice,
But complain that you've given it to them twice;
When you babble of putts you nearly holed,
By gad, sir,
You are getting old.

When for novels you lose your appetite
Because writers don't write what they used to write;
When by current art you are unbeguiled,
And pronounce it the work of an idiot child;
When cacophonous music leaves you cold,
By gad, sir,
You are getting old.

When you twist the sheets from night to morn
To recall when a cousin's daughter was born;
When youngsters mumble and won't speak up,
And your dog dodders, who was a pup;
When the modern girl seems a hussy bold,
By gad, sir,
You are getting old.

When you scoff at feminine fashion trends;
When strangers resemble absent friends;
When you start forgetting the neighbors' names
And remembering bygone football games;
When you only drop in at the club to scold,
By gad, sir,
You are getting old.

But when you roar at the income tax,
And the slippery bureaucratic hacks,
And the ancient political fishlike smell,
And assert that the world is going to hell,
Why you are not old at all, at all;
By gad, sir,
You are on the ball.

THE HAT'S GOT MY TONGUE

A girl, oh a girl is a wonderful thing,
And so I am happy to say is spring,
And a girl in spring is the absolute works
But for one conspicuous item that irks:
      That hat.
A girl in spring is a skylark's hymn,
An evensong in a cloister dim,
A moon in June and a dove in love,
But why the discordant detail above:
      That hat?
The crocuses put their best feet foremost,
The softest, tenderest raindrops pour most,
Nature walks forth in a robe of dawn,
And you, my love, what do you put on?
      That hat.
Purple the lilac and green the oaks,
Is spring the time for a milliner's hoax?
Your taste, methought, simply hibernated;
But what did I get when for spring I waited?
      That hat.
A girl, oh a girl is a wonderful thing,
And so I am happy to say is spring,
And you are what I adore the sight of;
That hat is what I adore you in spite of—
Take it off and let's jump on it!

Please don't anybody ask me to decide anything,
  I do not know a nut from a meg,
Or which came first, the lady or the tiger,
  or which came next, the chicken or the egg.
It takes a man of vision
To make a decision,
And my every memory
Is far too dilemmary.
I am, alas, to be reckoned
With the shortstop who can't decide whether to throw
  to first or second,
Nor can I decide whether to put, except after c,
E before i, or i before e.
But where this twilight mind really goes into eclipse
Is in the matter of tips.
I stand stricken before the triple doom,
Whether, and How Much, and Whom.
Tell me, which is more unpleasant,
The look from him who is superior to a tip and
  gets it, or from him who isn't and doesn't?
I had rather be discovered playing with my toes in
  the Boston Aquarium
Than decide wrongly about an honorarium.
Oh, to dwell forever amid Utopian scenery
Where hotels and restaurants and service stations are
  operated by untippable unoffendable machinery.

I'LL GLADLY PULL OVER TO THE CURB

If I have one outstanding desire
It is to know the answer to the question,
     Where's the fire?
Shall I tell you about my environs?
They are populated exclusively by alarums and sirens.
No wonder I flunked my secret agent course, when
     every time I tackled my cipher and code work,
Why, along came some hook-and-ladder on its
     road work.
The engines hoot by, a dozen times per diem,
And to me it's Mysterious, and Mysterious with a big
     M, not a wee m,
Because no matter how desperately I try to,
I can never spot hide or hair of the fires
     they are hooting by to.
I am dazed, please do not criticize my daze;
I guess I have heard a million fire engines hoot by, yet
     I have never seen so much as a doghouse ablaze.
Firemen, what is your destination?
Is there really a conflagration?
You have lickety-splitted by so often that my
     thoughts are utterly split-licketed;
I don't believe there ever was a fire, I believe
     I'm just being picketed.

Just imagine yourself seated on a shadowy terrace,
And beside you is a girl who stirs you more
strangely than an heiress.
It is a summer evening at its most superb,
And the moonlight reminds you that To Love
is an active verb,
And your hand clasps hers, which rests there
without shrinking,
And after a silence fraught with romance you ask her
what she is thinking,
And she starts and returns from the moon-washed
distances to the shadowy veranda,
And says, Oh I was wondering how many bamboo
shoots a day it takes to feed a baby Giant Panda.
Or you stand with her on a hilltop and gaze
on a winter sunset,
And everything is as starkly beautiful as a page
from Sigrid Undset,
And your arm goes round her waist and you make
an avowal which for masterfully marshaled
emotional content might have been a page of
Ouida's or Thackeray's,
And after a silence fraught with romance she says,
I forgot to order the limes for the Daiquiris.
Or in a twilight drawing room you have just asked
the most momentous of questions,

And after a silence fraught with romance she says,
    I think this little table would look better
    where that little table is, but then where would
    that little table go, have you any suggestions?
And that's the way they go around hitting below
    our belts;
It isn't that nothing is sacred to them, it's just
    that at the Sacred Moment they are always
    thinking of something else.

THE BUSES HEADED FOR SCRANTON

The buses headed for Scranton travel in pairs.
The lead bus is the bolder,
With the taut appearance of one who greatly dares;
The driver glances constantly over his shoulder.

The buses headed for Scranton are sturdy craft,
Heavy-chested and chunky;
They have ample vision sideways and fore and aft;
The passengers brave, the pilots artful and spunky.

Children creep hand in hand up gloomy stairs;
The buses headed for Scranton travel in pairs.

They tell of a bus that headed for Scranton alone;
It dwindled into the West.
It was later found near a gasoline pump—moss-grown,
Deserted, abandoned, like the *Mary Celeste*.

Valises snuggled trimly upon the racks,
Lunches in tidy packets,
Twelve *Daily Newses* in neat, pathetic stacks,
Thermoses, Chiclets, and books with paper jackets.

Some say the travelers saw the Wendigo,
Or were eaten by bears.
I know not the horrid answer, I only know
That the buses headed for Scranton travel in pairs.

OAFISHNESS SELLS GOOD, LIKE AN ADVERTISEMENT SHOULD

I guess it is farewell to grammatical compunction,
I guess a preposition is the same as a conjunction,
I guess an adjective is the same as an adverb,
And "to parse" is a bad verb.
Blow, blow, thou winter wind,
Thou are not that unkind
Like man's ingratitude to his ancestors
    who left him the English language
    for an inheritance;
This is a chromium world in which even the Copley
    Plazas and the Blackstones and the Book Cadillacs
    are simplified into Sheratons.
I guess our ancient speech has gone so flat
    that we have to spike it;
Like the hart panteth for the water brooks I pant
    for a revival of Shakespeare's *Like You Like It.*
I can see the tense draftees relax and purr
When the sergeant barks, "Like you were."
—And don't try to tell me that our well has been
    defiled by immigration;
Like goes Madison Avenue; like goes the nation.

LATHER AS YOU GO

Beneath this slab
John Brown is stowed.
He watched the ads,
And not the road.

THE BARGAIN

As I was going to St. Ives
I met a man with seven lives;
Seven lives,
In seven sacks,
Like seven beeves
On seven racks.
These seven lives
He offered to sell,
But which was best
He couldn't tell.
He swore that with any
I'd be happy forever;
I bought all seven
And thought I was clever,
But his parting words
I can't forget:
Forever
Isn't over yet.

How simple was the relationship between the sexes
    in the days of Francesca di Rimini;
Men were menacing, women were womeny.
When confronted with women, men weren't
    expected to understand them;
Their alternatives were, if rejected, to un-hand,
    and if accepted, to hand them.
I attribute much of our modern tension
To a misguided striving for intersexual comprehensio
It's about time to realize, brethren, as best we can,
That a woman is not just a female man.
How bootless, then, to chafe
When they are late because they have no watch
    with them, all eleven of their watches are on the
    dressing table or in the safe;
Give your tongue to the cat
When you ask what they want for their birthday
    and they say, Oh anything, and you get anything,
    and then discover it should have been anything
    but that.
Pocket the gold, fellows, ask not why it glisters;
As Margaret Fuller accepted the universe,
    so let us accept her sisters.
Women would I think be easier nationalized
Than rationalized,

And the battle of the sexes can be a most
    enjoyable scrimmage
If you'll only stop trying to create woman
    in your own image.

MORE ABOUT PEOPLE

When people aren't asking questions
They're making suggestions
And when they're not doing one of those
They're either looking over your shoulder
    or stepping on your toes
And then as if that weren't enough to annoy you
They employ you.
Anybody at leisure
Incurs everybody's displeasure.
It seems to be very irking
To people at work to see other people not working,
So they tell you that work is wonderful medicine,
Just look at Firestone and Ford and Edison,
And they lecture you till they're out of breath
    or something
And then if you don't succumb they starve you
    to death or something.
All of which results in a nasty quirk:
That if you don't want to work you have to work
    to earn enough money so that you won't have
    to work.

WILL CONSIDER SITUATION

These here are words of radical advice
    for a young man looking for a job;
Young man, be a snob.
Yes, if you are in search of arguments against
    starting at the bottom,
Why I've gottom.
Let the personnel managers differ;
It's obvious that you will get on faster at the top
    than at the bottom because there are more people
    at the bottom than at the top so naturally
    the competition at the bottom is stiffer.
If you need any further proof that my theory works,
Well, nobody can deny that presidents get paid more
    than vice-presidents and vice-presidents
    get paid more than clerks.
Stop looking at me quizzically;
I want to add that you will never achieve fortune
    in a job that makes you uncomfortable physically.
When anybody tells you that hard jobs are better
    for you than soft jobs be sure to repeat this
    text to them,
Postmen tramp around all day through rain and snow
    just to deliver people's in cozy air-conditioned
    offices checks to them.
You don't need to interpret tea leaves stuck in a cup

To understand that people who work sitting down
  get paid more than people who work standing up.
Another thing about having a comfortable job is
  you not only accumulate more treasure;
You get more leisure.
So that when you find you have worked so
  comfortably that your waistline is a menace,
You correct it with golf or tennis.
Whereas if in an uncomfortable job like piano-moving
  or stevedoring you indulge,
You have no time to exercise, you just continue
  to bulge.
To sum it up, young man, there is every reason
  to refuse a job that will make heavy demands
  on you corporally or manually,
And the only intelligent way to start your career
  is to accept a sitting position paying
  at least twenty-five thousand dollars annually.

SONG FOR DITHERERS

I journey not whence nor whither,
I languish alone in a dither;
I journey not to nor fro,
And my dither to me I owe.
I could find a pleasanter name for it
Had I somebody else to blame for it,
But alas that beneath the sun
Dithers are built for one.
This is the song of the dither,
For viol, bassoon or zither,
Till the greenest simpletons wither
This is the song of the dither;
When regular troubles are wrong with you,
Others are guilty along with you;
Dithers are private trouble
Where you privately stew and bubble.
Come hither, somebody, come hither,
Would you care for a share of my dither?
I want somebody else to be mad at;
"Have at you!" to cry, and be had at.
I am tired of being angry at me,
There is room in my dither for three,
There is room in my dither for two;
We could butt at each other and moo;
We could hiss like the serpent, and slither
Through the tropical depths of my dither;

Like bees we could fight along beelines,
Or spit at each other like felines;
I care not who gaineth the laurel,
All I want is a foe and a quarrel.
Alone in my dither I pine.
For the sake of the days of lang syne,
For your white-haired old feyther and mither,
Come along, come along to my dither.
With no foe in my dither but me,
I swoon, I lay doon, and I dee.

SONG OF THE OPEN ROAD

I think that I shall never see
A billboard lovely as a tree.
Indeed, unless the billboards fall
I'll never see a tree at all.

THE CANTALOUPE

One cantaloupe is ripe and lush,
Another's green, another's mush.
I'd buy a lot more cantaloupe
If I possessed a fluoroscope.

I do not like the winter wind
That whistles from the North.
My upper teeth and those beneath,
They jitter bàck and forth.
Oh, some are hanged, and some are skinned,
And others face the winter wind.

I do not like the summer sun
That scorches the horizon.
Though some delight in Fahrenheit,
To me it's deadly pizen.
I think that life would be more fun
Without the simmering summer sun.

I do not like the signs of spring,
The fever and the chills,
The icy mud, the puny bud,
The frozen daffodils.
Let other poets gayly sing;
I do not like the signs of spring.

I do not like the foggy fall
That strips the maples bare;
The radiator's mating call,
The dank, rheumatic air.
I fear that taken all in all,
I do not like the foggy fall.

The winter sun, of course, is kind,
And summer wind's a savior,
And I'll merrily sing of fall and spring
When they're on their good behavior.
But otherwise I see no reason
To speak in praise of any season.

THE PARSNIP

The parsnip, children, I repeat,
Is simply an anemic beet.
Some people call the parsnip edible;
Myself, I find this claim incredible.

THE MERMAID

Say not the mermaid is a myth,
I knew one once named Mrs. Smith.
She stood while playing cards or knitting;
Mermaids are not equipped for sitting.

Set in Monotype Walbaum, a light, open typeface designed
by Justus Erich Walbaum (1768-1839), who was a type
founder at Goslar and at Weimar.

Printed on Hallmark Eggshell Book paper.

Designed by Harald Peter.

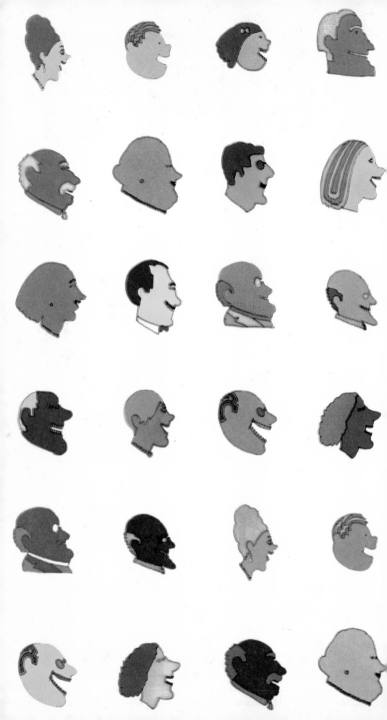